Depression.... A Guide for Caregivers

By

Gary Austin Kochenberger, PhD

ISBN: 1468135058
ISBN-13: 9781468135053

Depression.... A Guide for Caregivers

About the Author:

Gary Kochenberger was born and raised in Pueblo, Colorado. He went to college at the University of Colorado where he took a degree in electrical engineering and then a PhD in Management Science. He is currently a professor of Decision Science at the University of Colorado at Denver.

He met his wife, Ann, in grade school and they were married in 1960 right out of high school. Ann suffered with various levels of depression on and off for more than 30 years. Some of her bouts were very severe and took her to the brink of suicide. Throughout her struggles, Gary was the one constant in her life she could count on. In assuming the role as Ann's caregiver, Gary read books and articles about depression, went to therapy sessions, and generally did whatever was required to help Ann survive her darkest days. His experiences with Ann and the research he conducted to prepare for his caregiver role are distilled into his book *Depression...a Guide for Caregivers.*

Cover photo courtesy of Reveille Wright Kennedy, artist, photographer.

Preface:

This book is intended for non-professionals who find themselves thrust into the role of a caregiver for someone who is suffering with depression. Fortunately, there are many well-trained mental health professionals today who are available to "officially" provide aid and comfort to those who are depressed. These professionals provide medications and therapy, vitally important components of any effective treatment. What happens minute by minute during the lonely struggle in the absence of the trained professional, however, depends on a host of other factors that collectively comprise a broader package of support. A key part of this broader support group is often a spouse, parent, child, sibling, or close friend who finds themselves compelled to assume the role of a non-professional caregiver. In many cases, their role is as important as that of the pros. It is for these folks that this book is intended.

I've kept this book short and to the point because I know how busy you are. My goal was to produce a guide for caregivers that was easy and quick to read yet informative. Note that I've included an appendix that contains information about additional resources as well as a glossary of important terms related to mental illness and depression. The more you know about the subject, the more effective you'll be in your role as a caregiver.

Gary A. Kochenberger

CONTENTS

Chapter 1: Introduction

Unfortunately, everyone knows someone who is depressed. Whether or not they are officially diagnosed, they are functionally impaired as they struggle to cope with the overbearing influence and control the depression imposes. This illness is enormously powerful, having the ability to take an emotionally healthy person and turn them into a mere shadow of their healthy self—into a listless person of low self esteem and void of ambition. In the most severe cases, the depressed person may be incapable of doing the most basic simple tasks. They desperately need your help!

My wife, Ann, has suffered with severe depression on and off for more than 30 years. In her darkest and most challenging episodes, she had suicidal tendencies and on a couple of occasions came very close to ending her life. For a variety of reasons she never carried through with this act of self destruction, and over time she learned not only how to cope with her depression but how to return to the emotionally healthy life she had in her pre-depression days. The complete story of Ann's struggles and her recovery is told in her book Out of Focus....Again: A Journey from Depression to Recovery Through Courage, Love and Commitment. Her book shares valuable lessons that are useful for both caregivers and those who are depressed.

I was at Ann's side throughout the ups, downs, and countless challenges she faced with her depression. As her husband and best friend, I became her caregiver. We walked the long road to recovery together. We were often confused, frustrated, and unsure of where we were headed and what the outcome might be. But, we were in it together and we were determined to deal with it as best we could. Ann's story had a happy ending. Today Ann is emotionally healthy; once again a vibrant, self-assured, fulfilled person.

During Ann's journey to recovery, I discovered my role as caregiver on the fly. I had no formal training in this arena. But I had love, commitment and a relentless resolve to "keep going" that played a much-needed role. I'm writing this book to share my experiences and the lessons I learned researching the topic of depression that helped Ann get through some really difficult times. I hope that some of my experiences will be useful to others who find themselves in the role of a caregiver. It is a difficult, frustrating role to play. But, it is terribly important and can help considerably to mitigate the devastation of depression. In really severe cases, it can make the difference between life and death.

Chapter 2: Recognizing Depression

We weren't sure what we were dealing with when depression first entered our lives. Ann was in her early 30s and by all accounts had a wonderful life. We had a strong marriage, two healthy children, a good income, a supportive family, and a substantial network of friends. Yet Ann was having feelings of self-doubt. Something new and unsettling was going on and these feelings soon led to withdrawal from friends and activities, intensified feeling of helplessness and hopelessness, and, eventually, full-blown, debilitating depression.

In the beginning Ann was confused about what was happening to her. As her feeling of self-doubt persisted, she made an appointment with our family doctor who told her she was showing signs of depression, gave her a prescription for an anti-depressant, and recommended that she start therapy sessions with a local psychologist. Despite our closeness, Ann kept all this from me for several weeks. She was confused and embarrassed. It was after several therapy sessions that she explained to me what she was doing and brought me into her new world. It was at this point that I realized how serious things might become. This was the beginning of my 30+-year job as Ann's caregiver. Her symptoms, which were to become much more severe in later years, were relatively mild at this point. My tenure as her caregiver started before many of the classical sign of depression were on display. Unfortunately they would show up later.

Many caregivers are thrust into action with a loved one or close friend who is already fully and severely depressed. Yet many of us outside of the mental health community are not familiar with the telltale signs of depression. We've all been emotionally down from time to time, a bit blue perhaps. But there is a huge difference between being a little blue and being seriously depressed. Basically the difference has to do with both the intensity and duration of the feelings. People quickly rebound from a bout of the blues. Depression, on the other hand, if left untreated, can last indefinitely and will likely get worse over time.

A seriously depressed individual typically has persistent feelings of sadness, loneliness, hopelessness and worthlessness. It's common for them to lose interest in friends and activities they once enjoyed. They may have difficulty making even simple decisions...they are simply not capable. They withdraw from their earlier healthy life into a dark, inner-focused, confused world filled with despair where they often have thoughts of death and suicide. In many ways, they are a substantially different person than the healthy person you knew previously.

Sometimes the emotional degradation is accompanied by physical symptoms such as too little or too much sleep, weight gain or loss, and lack of energy and ambition. Muscle aches and headaches are also fairly common symptoms. The good news is that effective treatments for depression are available today. Moreover, the stigma of mental illness is no longer what it once was as people now talk openly about this affliction. The likelihood of recovery, with appropriate treatment, has never been greater.

Chapter 3: What Causes Depression

Universities and other research laboratories around the world are gaining new insights into depression and its possible causes. At this point, however, there is no definitive understanding of what causes depression. It's widely believed that depression is a disease of the brain caused by a chemical imbalance. Much of the medication prescribed for depression is intended to address this imbalance. It's not known with certainty, however, what causes the chemical imbalance.

Popular theories regarding the cause of the imbalance include heredity, which may set up a predisposition for depression, and external events that negatively impact one's life. Examples of such events would include such things as the death of a family member or friend, a divorce, the loss of a job, or a friend moving away. Lesser events, like the loss of a pet or a significant disappointment of some kind can also serve as a catalyst ushering in a bout of depression. In general, any significant negative change in one's life can function as a contributing or launching event.

Many professionals believe that those who are mildly depressed or pre-disposed to be depressed can become severely depressed due to such "triggering" events. The chemistry of the brain and these influential events seem to be mutually re-enforcing, leading to a more severe level of depression.

A good example of a triggering event is the move my wife and I made from Colorado to Mississippi in 1999. Some 20 plus years after Ann first became depressed; she was at that time on a successful maintenance program of medication, therapy and a host of other supportive activities resulting in her being mentally healthy. She was emotionally stable, happy, fulfilled, and by all accounts perfectly normal. Moreover, she had been this way for several years. It appeared that her days of being severely depressed were behind her.

Unexpectedly, I received an invitation to go to the University of Mississippi for a two-year period to start a new research center. Ole Miss had received a large amount of money from a private foundation for the purpose of establishing a research center and the plan was that I, along with another professor, would be the inaugural director. After the two-year period, we would return to our positions at the University of Colorado. This was a huge opportunity for me professionally.

Ann was excited for me and very supportive of the idea of the move. After all, it was just for two years; and, it would be an adventure giving us the opportunity to explore parts of the south we'd not seen before. Moreover, much of the last 20+ years had been spent "about Ann" as we single-mindedly focused on getting her well. Now that she was feeling well, Ann was eager to do something for me. We went ahead with the move, bought a house in Oxford, MS, where Ole Miss is located, and by all appearances seemed to settle in nicely to our new location. The first eight months were great. The job was everything I had anticipated and we were enjoying many new experiences in the south.

Ann tried really hard to make the best of our new situation. But once the excitement and novelty of the move wore off, she began to slip back into depression. She had been taken out of the familiar Denver location, where our children, grandchildren and her friends were. Despite efforts to meet new people and to get involved in volunteer work, Ann rapidly became overwhelmed with despair and loneliness. Toward the end of our first year in Oxford, Ann was once again in the grips of a major depression. This was perhaps her worst episode ever and once again she was on the verge of self-destruction with frequent thoughts of suicide.

Looking back it seems so clear. I had an exciting job that kept me busy and fulfilled. On the other hand, Ann had little to do and lots of time to think about all she was missing back home. She felt lonely and useless. Despite a continued regiment of medication and therapy, the move to Mississippi proved to be a disruption in Ann's safety net that she simply couldn't deal with. All the change

11

that the move brought into our lives proved to be a triggering event for a new round of depression. Given all that we had been through in the earlier years of Ann's depression and all that I'd read about over the years about depression, I should have seen this coming. We should have never moved to Mississippi. It almost cost Ann her life.

Triggering events don't have to be as extreme as the move described above. Any event perceived to be negative could be a catalyst leading to depression.

Chapter 4: Why me?

The short answer is: Because someone you care about desperately needs you! Nobody seeks out this assignment. It's a hand that is dealt us and we need to rise to the challenge. Of course, this is easier said than done.

In terms of formal training, I was ill prepared to be a caregiver. My education was in engineering, mathematics and business. I knew precious little about mental health and all the "depression – related" topics I would soon become familiar with. I knew nothing about psychotherapy but doubted if it was ever necessary. As I saw what was happening to Ann, I knew that I had to be there for her. And, this meant that I had to learn what I could about her illness. I had to read about depression, talk with and learn from mental health professionals, and join Ann, as appropriate, in going to therapy sessions. On this later point I did a 180-degree switch. Seeing how psychotherapy helped Ann, I rapidly became converted as I recognized the positive role it was playing in Ann's treatment. You couldn't find a stronger proponent of psychotherapy than I am today.

The ideal, well-prepared caregiver may exist but is most likely very rare. People like me, initially clueless about depression, are probably the rule rather than the exception. Fortunately, lacking formal mental health training does not rule anyone out. The key requirements are simple---and most of us have them: namely, we need to "be there" and help as best we can. I illustrate this in the chapters that follow.

Chapter 5: How to Help

You are not a substitute for mental health professionals. Rather, you are in a support role, with the important objective of supplementing and re-enforcing the help provided by physicians and other mental health professionals. To carry out this role, you need to educate yourself about depression. For this purpose there are lots of materials available from mental health professionals, in print form (books and articles), and for reading on the Internet. In the appendix of this book I give a list of such materials along with a glossary of mental health terms. I recommend that you take these as a starting point for your continuing education about depression.

It is really important that you acknowledge the seriousness of the illness and that you don't in any way discount what the depressed person is struggling with. Nobody chooses to be depressed. Yet, the strongest among us can succumb to it. The one you are caring for needs to know that you understand that they are in the grips of something powerful and that you are going to help them as they struggle to cope and to get better---and that they can in fact get better!

You need to help them understand the importance of medication, therapy, and other components of a complete coping package. Usually an entire package is more effective that a single component.   The conventional wisdom is that depression is a disease of the brain and most people suffering with depression will respond positively to appropriate medication. Unfortunately, determining the right medication is far from an exact science. As a caregiver, you don't need to be an expert on medication but you need to know that for most patients appropriate medication is an indispensible part of the recovery process. Moreover, you need to know that there are lots of different kinds of drugs for depression; and that these drugs differ in their effectiveness for different types of depression. Furthermore, they differ in effectiveness from person to person for the same type of depression.

And if that's not frustrating enough, you need to know that determining the best medication and dosage for a given person is a process of trial and error where each trial may take three to six weeks to determine whether or not the current prescription is "right." And then there are the side effects…. like weight gain or loss, loss of sex drive, insomnia, dizziness, fatigue, and headaches. Medications can affect different patients in very different ways. Some people tolerate a given drug while experiencing significant side effects from other drugs. Finally, you need to know that the effectiveness of a particular medication may decline over time. This means that a workable medical solution at one point in time may not be the ideal medical solution some time later. Having the appropriate medication is an on-going process that requires frequent monitoring. Ann spoke often with her doctors about her medication and made changes as needed. She and I would discuss this issue as well and I always encouraged her to be proactive regarding her medication. It's up to the patient to make the assessment as to whether or not a given medication is providing the help that is needed and whether or not the side effects are acceptable. The caregiver can and should encourage such proactive involvement.

Note that only a physician (i.e., a medical doctor) can prescribe medications. A family doctor, while licensed to issue prescriptions, may or may not be an expert on depression and the various medications available for treating it. You and the person you are helping may have to do some homework here to make sure the appropriate medications have been prescribed. Moreover, you need to make sure they not only have the appropriate medication but that they continue to take it even when they start to feel better.

There are a variety of views on how long medication needs to be taken. Some patients simply don't like the idea of taking drugs; or, they are eager to discontinue taking their prescription due to the cost of the drugs and/or due to their side effects. As a caregiver, you need to advise against stopping the medication unless a doctor advises that it is safe to stop. The danger, of course, is that without medication, one could slip back into depression. In my wife's case, she plans on taking her medication for the rest of her life as she views her situation as being in a state of successful maintenance rather than being cured. Many others feel this way as well.

Psychotherapy, like medication, is usually a major part of any effective treatment plan and you need to encourage these counseling sessions in addition to medication. A severely depressed person just starting therapy sessions may have to be in session as frequently as once or more a week. Overtime, they can go less frequently. For instance, my wife, who has now been free of symptoms of depression for several years, sees her therapist once or twice a year. For the most part, these are not "deep" therapy sessions but rather are intended to simply review how things are going and to determine if any changes need to be made in the medications she is taking.

It's important to know that not all therapists are created equal and the depressed person you are caring for may have to try two or more before finding that special one with the appropriate level of comfort and trust. A suitable therapist could be a psychiatrist, psychologist, or an appropriately trained nurse practitioner. Most insurance policies now have provisions for both medication and counseling. Nonetheless there are costs involved. Unfortunately, getting appropriate help for depression is not cheap.

You need to have realistic expectations about counseling, what a good therapist can (and can't) do, and what time frame will likely be needed before significant progress is made. And, you need to help the person you are caring for to have these same realistic expectations. The basic role of psychotherapy is to help one discover why they are feeling the way they are and what some of the likely causes are. A skilled therapist will guide you through this process of self exploration, asking probing questions and encouraging you to look honestly and objectively into what is happening and why. The therapist won't have answers for your problems. Their job is to facilitate the discovery process leading to insights that come from within. They create a safe, risk-free environment (their office and their professional relationship with you) that enables this process to play out.

The time frame for realizing results from therapy sessions can vary significantly from person to person as it depends on several factors. For instance, it depends on such things as the severity of depression, medications being taken, the patient's attitude toward therapy, the skill and experience of the therapist, and the comfort level/trust that is built with the therapist. Given all these factors, there are no firm guidelines on how long a person needs to remain in counseling. Many feel, however, that for most depressed people, six to ten counseling sessions is a minimum number required begin to produce positive results. Many patients find therapy sessions to be so helpful that they continue with them, if only on an infrequent, maintenance schedule, indefinitely.

You need to encourage other coping strategies beyond medication and therapy sessions as well. I would include here such things are exercise, religion, interacting with friends, and perhaps starting to do some volunteer or other work. These later activities can help the depressed person feel better about themselves. Friends and work might not be viable options until substantial progress has been made, but exercise and religion are options that can be adopted at any point. All of these coping strategies played an important role in Ann's successful treatment over the years. It is important not to push any of these options prematurely. In time the support package should lead to improvement. But, until significant improvement is achieved, the depressed person may benefit most from your constant caring and attention. As they start to get better, you can encourage a broader set of activities.

You need to recognize that their ability to make decisions may be greatly diminished. Accordingly, the depressed person should postpone major decisions if at all possible. Seriously depressed people simply aren't rational. In many cases they are barely functioning at all. As caregiver you need to help guard against serious mistakes that might be made here. Until some level of success has been achieved via medication, therapy and possible other coping means, the depressed person may be incapable of even the simplest tasks—like getting out of bed in the morning, looking up a doctor's phone number, calling for an appointment, appropriately taking their medication, driving to an appointment, and so forth. You need to be prepared to assist in these activities. Otherwise they simply won't get done.

Note that this means that your role as a caregiver may expand to include that of serving as a patient advocate. In this regard, you'll be helping to navigate the often confusing medical system and generally serving as a liaison between the patient and the system of health care providers.

And be prepared to talk. A severely depressed person needs to hear from you, over and over again, that you are there for them and that they can and will get better. They are feeling empty, helpless, worthless, and defeated. Your goal in these talks is to give them hope.

There were many days when Ann and I would talk for hours. Typically I would do most of the talking. I would hold her, talk about the improvement that was going to come, tell her positive things about the children, and generally try to divert her from her otherwise negative thinking. In the absence of such diversions, Ann exaggerated the negative and minimized the positive in just about everything. As needed, we would go over and over the same discussions, day after day. Each time it was as if she hadn't heard it before---or, as if she just didn't believe it. In time, as she started to feel better, our conversations became more two sided and more adult like. But, there were stretches going on for months where we had these repetitive, parent/child like conversations. She needed them.

Once the medication, therapy and other components of the treatment package yields results and there is a return to normalcy, you need to remain on duty looking out for signs of slippage as well as being pro-active regarding the potential impact of new triggering events. You simply need to deal with these in an open, timely constructive manner as you have done with other aspects of your role as a caregiver.

It's important to acknowledge up front that you'll make some mistakes and not always be the perfect caregiver. That's ok...you'll still do just fine. I briefly touch on this topic in the next chapter.

Chapter 6: How Not to Help

There are lots of mistakes that can be encountered. I recounted in the previous chapter the very serious mistake I made in moving from Colorado to Mississippi. I totally underestimated the impact the move would have on Ann and the role it played as a major triggering event. Not all mistakes are as consequential as this one.

In your support role, for example, it is important to keep in mind the difference between being depressed and having the blues. What might be effective in addressing a case of the blues might be totally inappropriate and ineffective for depression. Early in my tenure as Ann's caregiver, scrambling as I was to help her cope and to achieve a more positive outlook on her life, I made a mistake regarding the role of positive thinking and the notion that happiness is a choice we can make. My daughter, a child of about 10 years old at the time, is quite artistic and I asked her to draw up a poster which we taped to our refrigerator that said "Happy Thoughts Make Happy People."

I'm pleased to report that my effectiveness as a caregiver grew substantially and rapidly after hitting this low point represented by the poster. I still believe in the importance of positive thinking and the idea that we can meet the normal ups and downs of day to day living by choosing to see the glass half full rather than half empty. But make no mistake: effectively treating depression is much more difficult than simply "choosing to by happy." Those suffering with severe depression are not simply going to snap out of it. And, their condition is not going to self-correct. No amount of wishful thinking will bring about such a miraculous transformation. Don't assume otherwise.

In your dealings as a caregiver, things won't always go smoothly. You'll need to choose your battles carefully so as to avoid the appearance of always being negative and controlling. Your eagerness to help them do the right thing puts you at risk here; and the appropriate handling of your relationship may prove to be more of an art than a science. Nonetheless, some fights are worth pursuing and it may be a mistake to give in on a certain issue just to avoid the possibility of a confrontation.

For example, a depressed person may not have a rational assessment of the progress their treatment plan is delivering. They may want, for instance, to give up on their medication or their therapy sessions prematurely because they have doubts about their effectiveness. Unless your informed assessment is in agreement with theirs, this could be an example of a fight worth fighting. Helping them come to a more rational perspective can be done without being confrontational. This takes time, energy and patience. But, it's likely a mistake to take the easy way out and tell them what they would like to hear.

All told, you are best equipped to help if you have reasonable expectations about the magnitude of the battle you are in and how to deal with it. This means that you should not underestimate the extent of the depression and the control is has on them. Moreover, you should not assume that upon feeling better, they will necessarily be free of depression forever. In fact, for people who have suffered several major bouts of depression, the word "recovery" may imply a return to an acceptable level of normalcy that can be managed by a continued treatment plan rather than meaning permanently cured. You should consult with mental health professionals before deciding whether or not the treatment plan that led to recovery needs to be maintained.

Chapter 7: Suicide

Nobody wants to talk about suicide. Yet, it's a solution that is commonly adopted by those who are severely depressed. It's been estimated that roughly one million people commit suicide each year. It's really important, then, that you are aware of the possibility and that you are on guard looking for signs that the person you are caring for is thinking about suicide. At such a point, even though it may be uncomfortable, you need to talk about it openly and directly. No beating around the bush here.

Having said that, I must admit that I was guilty for many years of not addressing this straight on. It was on my mind and I worried about how close Ann may have been to such an act. I would say things like "please don't ever hurt yourself" and she would nod in the affirmative. We understood each other but for some reason we couldn't bring ourselves to use the "S" word during the 20 years of Ann's depression. Later on this verbal prohibition passed and we talked more directly about suicide.

There are times when the severely depressed feel that they are out of options. Viable solutions either aren't available, so it seems, or they haven't delivered the relief that is needed. They can get in a state of lonely, inescapable hopelessness accompanied by the pain of it all. At such times, suicide may loom as the one available solution they could choose that would end their unbearable situation---that would give them the relief they are desperately seeking.

Ann talks in her book, *Out of Focus...Again,* about how in her darkest hours of depression she contemplated suicide on several occasions and how in the apparent absence of other options, suicide emerged as the only choice she could make that would bring her pain and suffering to an end. She took a semblance of comfort in the fact that there was one solution that she had the power to choose if things got too unbearable to endure.

As a caregiver, you need to be aware of the telltale warning signs of a potentially suicidal person. According to *Helpguide*, a non-profit resource for the mental health community, these signs include:

- A preoccupation with death...unusual focus on death, dying, or violence.
- Showing no hope for the future...feelings of helplessness, or being trapped.
- Exhibiting self-loathing or self-hatred...feelings of worthlessness, guilt, and shame.
- Becoming excessively isolated ...withdrawing from friends and family.

- Exhibiting self-destructive behavior...increased alcohol or drug use, reckless driving.
- Saying goodbye...putting affairs in order, giving away key possessions and saying goodbye in a manner indicating that they will not be seen again.
- The sudden gathering of lethal means...seeking access to pills, guns, and other objects that could be used in a suicide attempt.

These signs, along with any talk about suicide, should be taken seriously and you should operate on the assumption that the one you are caring for is in fact thinking about committing suicide. Your response should be to tackle this head on with frank discussions acknowledging their desperation, talking about other alternatives and how much you and others care about them, and generally trying to give them the glimmer of hope needed to enable them to continue the fight. They need to see a solution other than suicide. They may have a plan in mind. Your job is to disrupt the plan, buy some time, and continue to work toward helping them see another way out of the pain and hopelessness that has taken them to the brink of self-destruction.

If you are going to error here, it's best to error on the side of assuming a plan is in place and to be proactive in your efforts to disrupt it. In this regard, I used to talk with Ann about important coming family events because family events were always so important to her. I learned later from Ann that these efforts were effective. While she had suicidal plans, they didn't necessarily have a firm time frame for implementation and if something happened during the day to change her outlook, she simply put the suicide plans on the back burner where they remained as an option for a future day. This disruptive intervention usually had something to do with the family but in some cases was as simple as an unexpected call from an old friend or a smile from one of our children. Regardless, she remained alive.

For further assistance regarding suicide, call a suicide prevention hotline. For instance, the National Suicide Prevention Hotline at 1-800-273-8255 is a good source to turn to. Many communities have local hotlines available as well. Be proactive here. Find a suitable phone number, write it down and keep it handy.

Chapter 8: Caring for the caregiver

In recent years Ann and I have been giving joint presentations about her experiences with depression to various mental health groups. At these events, Ann is the main speaker but I always give a short talk about my perspective on her illness. During Q&A at one of the talks a member of the audience commented "I understand from Ann's presentation that you played a major role over the years helping her cope with her depression. I wonder, though, who took care of the caregiver"? As strange as this may sound, this was the first I had thought about it.

The answer regarding who took care of me is... "I did." Ann's illness had changed our relationship such that there were substantial periods of time where much of the parenting responsibilities became mine alone. Moreover I had Ann to care for and I had a career to pursue. In short, I was too busy to worry about whether or not I needed help. There were many times when I felt frustrated and unsure about how I should be handling the children or helping Ann with a certain issue. And there were times when the attention Ann needed from me as her caregiver took away substantially from time that I should have been devoting to my career.

Fortunately I had been to a few therapy sessions with Ann and these helped me to understand the magnitude of what we were dealing with and how I might help. Moreover, I was reading about mental health and depression in an effort to better prepare myself for the task at hand. In a very real manner, without thinking about it explicitly, I provided the help that I needed. Without ever talking about Ann's situation, I nonetheless did a pretty good job of keeping up my personal relationships with co-workers and I managed to keep up a fairly reliable regiment of exercise. Luckily my job was very flexible and I found the time to pursue my career in spite of the other responsibilities I was shouldering.

As I look back on it I see the one thing that would have helped me considerably would have been someone I could have confided in. I had several close friends who were good candidates for this but in the 70s and 80s people didn't talk openly about depression. And, Ann felt very strongly that her illness was private and not to be talked about. It seems clear to me now that I should have turned to therapy sessions for a safe haven for such discussions. As open as I became to Ann's involvement in therapy, it never occurred to me that I too could have benefited from therapy. I could have.

Things are much different today regarding the acceptance of depression as a common illness that afflicts many terrific people. Today we can talk much more openly about this illness and what needs to be done to help those who are suffering. Recalling as I have that I didn't have an explicit plan in place to care for me as a caregiver, I can list nonetheless a few elements of care that I'd recommend for caregivers today due to the extraordinary pressures they may be feeling. My recommendations for the successful care and feeding of today's caregivers are:

- Learn all you reasonably can about depression...this will make you a better caregiver and it will make you feel good about yourself in this role.

- Take time to take care of yourself...you don't need a lecture from me about diet and exercise. But, it's important not to get run down physically or emotionally. Healthy eating and exercise can help considerably in this regard.

- Don't be afraid to reach out for support...have someone you can turn to for discussions about not only aspects of depression but also about changes in relationships, parenting, career, and other issues now in your life because you are a caregiver. This could involve anyone from a trusted friend to a professional therapist.

- Don't be too hard on yourself...you won't always have the perfect response to every situation and there will be times when it might appear to you that you could have handled things differently. Try your best and overall you'll do just fine.

Be thankful...this is one of the most important jobs you'll ever have, and most likely among the most difficult. As challenging as the task may be, you should be thankful that you are in a position to help. This perspective, as opposed to "why me" will make it easier to carry on during the many trying times....and, it will create a lot of good Karma you can cash in on later.

Chapter 9: Summary

If you find yourself in the role of a caregiver, you've got a full plate! Presumably you already had a life before all this happened and now you have piled on top of an already busy life this incredibly difficult and time-consuming responsibility of being a caregiver. In the preceding chapters I've given you some guidance regarding making your care-giving activities as fruitful as possible. As you can see, there is a lot one can do to bone-up for the task at hand. The importance of your role will, at times, appear overwhelming. Although there is much to learn and to think about, the most important advice I can give you is to simply "be there" with unwavering support. There will be times when you are feeling frustrated, inadequate, angry and/or confused. I had these feelings often. Yet, it's not only possible but it's essential that you continue on...that you continue to "be there." For these challenging times, I suggest you adopt the mantra that sustained me throughout my many years as a caregiver: "Love never stops, love never gives up."

Appendix: Other Resources

It's really important that caregivers educates them self as much as possible about depression. Short of actually being depressed, I'm not sure anyone can fully understand how debilitating this disease can be….but, caregivers need to do the best they can to understand it and the irrational behavior it causes. Fortunately there are many resources available today to assist with this process of self-education. These materials consist primarily of books, articles, web sites, and support groups. Below I list some prominent resources that you may find helpful. Besides referring to the resources given below, I recommend that you seek out additional information by asking your doctor for recommendations, browsing through the self-help section of the library, and searching the web for new resources. I regularly Google some variation of a phrase like "helping those who are depressed." It's amazing how much new and useful information is available.

Books: There are many good books available for caregivers to read. Those listed below are highly recommended. They can be found in any major bookstore or ordered online from Amazon.

- *Out of Focus...Again: A journey from Depression to Recovery Through Courage, Love and Commitment,* by Ann Kochenberger
- *The Noonday Demon: An Atlas of Depression,* by Andrew Solomon
- *Undoing Depression,* by Richard O'Connor
- *Against Depression,* by Peter Kramer
- *Breaking the Patterns of Depression,* by Michael Yapko
- *Feeling Good: The New Mood Therapy,* by David Burns
- *Depression for Dummies,* by Laura Smith & Charles Elliott
- *What to do When Someone You Love is Depressed,* by Mitch Golant & Susan Golant

Important Organizations: Several national as well as local organizations exist that provide useful services to those who are depressed and to caregivers. Some of the key national organizations are listed below. You can visit them on the Internet to learn about the breath of services they provide. (Simply Google their name).

- National Alliance of Mental Illness (NAMI)
- Depression and Bipolar Support Alliance
- The Jed Foundation
- MedlinePlus
- National Council for Community Behavioral Healthcare

- Families for Depression Awareness
- Mental Health America
- National Hopeline Network
- National Institute of Mental Health (NIMH)

Web Sites: A variety of web sites are available providing a wide range of services. I recommend you visit some or all of the following.

- http://helpguide.org
- http://www.webmd.com
- http://www.dbsalliance.org
- http://familyaware.org
- http://avoiddepression.com
- http://medlineplus.gov
- http://www.healthyplace.com
- http://www.mayoclinic.com
- http://my.clevelandclinic.org
- http://www.nimh.nih.gov

Support Groups: Many communities have support groups sponsored by both local and national organizations that meet face to face on a regular basis like once a week. Information about these groups can be obtained from local mental health organizations as well as the Internet. Increasingly people are joining groups that meet on the Internet rather than face to face. Internet groups offer convenience and a level of anonymity that are important to many. Note that some groups are free while others charge a fee. Note also that some are sponsored by particular medications while others have no such affiliation. If you are just starting to look into the notion of a support group, I recommend that you visit the Mayo Clinic site

(http://www.mayoclinic.com/health/support-groups/MH00044) which is a good resource giving an overview of support groups in general. Beyond that, you might want to visit the websites of some of the organizations listed above and follow their link to support groups. For instance, the National Alliance on Mental Illness, the Depression and Bipolar Support Alliance, and Mental Health America all offer support group services. A Google search for "support groups for depression" will lead you to many others as well.

Glossary:

When I first started to educate myself about depression, I was not familiar with many of the terms that are a part of the mental health field. To help you in this regard, I'm including the following glossary of terms. Note that his glossary is adapted from http:/www.webmd.com.

- **Antidepressant:** A drug used to treat depression.

- **Anxiety disorder:** A chronic condition that causes anxiety so severe that it interferes with your life. Some people with depression also have an anxiety disorder.

- **Bipolar disorder:** A type of depression that causes mood swings between depression and mania.

- **Dysthymia:** A type of chronic depression that is less severe than major depression. It can last for years and prevent one from functionally normally.

- **Major depression:** The medical diagnosis for depression that lasts for at least two weeks and interferes with daily life. It causes symptoms like low energy, fatigue, and hopelessness.

- **Mania:** A period of intense happiness, irritability, or recklessness so extreme that it interferes with a person's life. A symptom of bipolar disorder.

- **Mood stabilizers:** A class of drugs used to treat some types of depression, like bipolar disorder.

- **Neurotransmitter:** A chemical in the brain, like serotonin or norepinphrine, that sends messages between brain cells. Medicines that treat depression often alter the levels of these chemicals.

- **Psychotherapy:** A way of treating a mental or emotional disorder by talking with a therapist.

- **Psychologist:** A professional who specializes in the treatment of mental or emotional disorders, usually through psychotherapy.

- **Psychiatrist:** A medical doctor who specializes in treating psychological disorders. They can prescribe drugs like antidepressants. They often use psychotherapy as well to treat depression.

ABOUT THE AUTHOR

Gary Kochenberger was born and raised in Pueblo, Colorado. He went to college at the University of Colorado where he took a degree in electrical engineering and then a PhD in Management Science. He is currently a professor of Decision Science at the University of Colorado at Denver.

He met his wife, Ann, in grade school and they were married in 1960 right out of high school. Ann suffered with various levels of depression on and off for more than 30 years. Some of her bouts were very severe and took her to the brink of suicide. Throughout her struggles, Gary was the one constant in her life she could count on. In assuming the role as Ann's caregiver, Gary read books and articles about depression, went to therapy sessions, and generally did whatever was required to help Ann survive her darkest days. His experiences with Ann and the research he conducted to prepare for his caregiver role are distilled into his book *Depression...a Guide for Caregivers.*

www.ingramcontent.com/pod-product-compliance
Lightning Source LLC
Chambersburg PA
CBHW070232290526
45789CB00004B/1592